# Day Tours
# in the
# east of Dorset

### Robert Westwood
robert.westwood3@btinternet.com

First published in 2006 by:
*Inspiring Places Publishing*
2 Down Lodge Close
Alderholt
Fordingbridge
Hampshire
SP63JA

ISBN 978-0-9552061-2-2
ISBN 0-9552061-2-X [10 digit]

Printed by ACH Colour, Bournemouth

*Inspiring Place*

204544321 P

# Contents:

*Above: Looking across Chapman's Pool from St. Aldhelm's Head.*

*Below right: Corfe Castle seen from Corfe Common.*

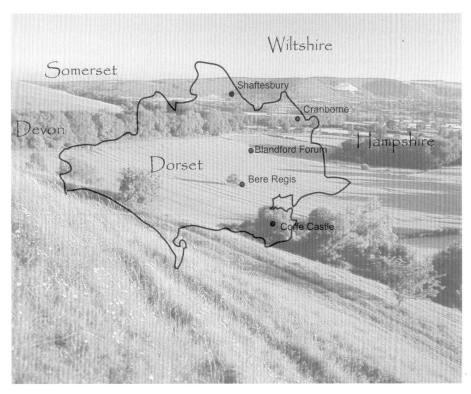

*Day Tours in the east of Dorset*

# Introduction

What makes a good day out? These days the leisure industry seems to grow and grow. There are numerous ways to relax and to be adventurous. Despite the development of theme parks and large entertainment centres the British countryside continues to draw visitors in their thousands. But what do you do when you go for a day out? This book will help you decide.

Most visitors to the countryside want to see its natural beauty and perhaps walk or picnic in picturesque surroundings. Many want to explore historical sites and interesting villages. Perhaps the day will be rounded off with a visit to a country pub or with a traditional cream tea. Many too will have their enjoyment enhanced by learning a little of the history of the area and of great events that have happened there.

This guide is for those people who want a relaxing and interesting day out in beautiful surroundings. It is divided into a number of tours each centred around a town or village. They can be used in a number of ways. Following each tour will give a varied and full day out, with chances to relax, to walk and to investigate interesting sites. Some people may wish to explore more fully or to do more walking, in which case not all the sites will be visited in the day. Alternatively, just use the guide for suggestions where to go.

*Day Tours in the east of Dorset*

# Tour 1 - Cranborne

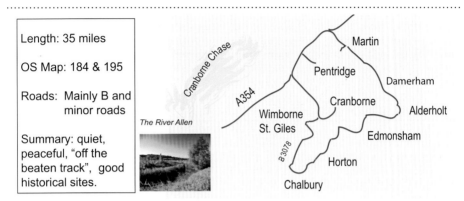

Length: 35 miles

OS Map: 184 & 195

Roads: Mainly B and minor roads

Summary: quiet, peaceful, "off the beaten track", good historical sites.

Cranborne Chase
Martin
Pentridge
Damerham
A354
Cranborne
Alderholt
The River Allen
Wimborne St. Giles
Edmonsham
B3078
Horton
Chalbury

Our first tour is about 35 miles in length. It can easily be done in a day with plenty of time to get out and explore the sites suggested, and to stop in one of the eating places. It could also be done in an afternoon, perhaps stopping for several short walks and ending in a pub or restaurant. It is a tour that takes in many less well known places of interest and so is somewhat off the "tourist track".

We start in the ancient village of Cranborne, lying at the eastern edge of the "chase" it gives its name to. Now a sleepy, yet thriving village, it was once a bustling market town, often thronged with troops guarding kings who hunted in the royal forests of the Chase; a custom started by King John who built a royal residence here.

The manor, home to Viscount Cranborne, is a wonderful example of an English country house. Dating from the time of Henry VIII, it was greatly improved by Robert Cecil who was given the estate by James I. The manor can be viewed from the front through its fine avenue of trees or from the rear by a footpath starting behind the church.

Leave Cranborne via the B3081 towards Sixpenny Handley. The route offers stunning views of the chalk farmland. Just before the junction with the A354, park at the side of the road and you will see the impressive remains of the Roman road [Ackling Dyke], instantly recognisable due to its dead straight course. This was one of a number of roads that enabled legions to move swiftly from their ships in Poole Harbour to garrisons all over southern England.

Follow the Blandford road north for a short distance then take the right turn signposted Pentridge. This is a dead end that leads only to the quiet, ancient little village. As well as simply absorbing the tranquility of this place, it is worth a short walk up to the hillfort at Penbury Knoll. Park near the small church; the footpath starts a little further down the road on the left. This is a splendid place for a picnic, with plenty of shade and wonderful views.

Penbury is one of many Iron Age hillforts scattered all over Dorset. Most were built from around 600-100 BC and were probably the fortresses of local chieftains. Roman sources record over twenty battles at hillforts in the campaign following the invasion of AD 43.

Return to the main Blandford road [A354] and continue towards Blandford. After about 2 miles turn right to the village of Martin. Turn right at the small village green with its antique pump and follow the road until it ends at the nature reserve of Martin Down, a wonderful piece of unspoilt chalk downland. A number of paths lead towards the ridge which is topped by the Romano-British earthwork known as Bokerley Dyke and marks the boundary between Dorset and Hampshire. Thought to have been built as a defence against Saxon invaders, it may have been overcome shortly before the decisive battle of Mount Badon which gave the Britons fifty years more peace. Who knows, Arthur himself may have stood atop this rampart!

Return to the village green and continue to Damerham, a charming village with a Saxon church. Take the road to Fordingbridge and after a while turn right to Alderholt, back in Dorset. You will pass Alderholt Mill, still producing fine quality flour and open for cream teas at weekends. Drive through Alderholt then turn left towards Verwood and then right to Edmonsham. Here is a fine Tudor manor house, owned by the same family since the 16th century. The gardens are open Sundays and Wednesdays throughout the summer and the house is open on Bank Holiday Mondays and Wednesdays during October.

Turn left in the village and follow the signs to Ringwood. In just over a mile turn right towards Woodlands and Horton. Horton is a delightful village with a lovely

_Knowlton Church and its Neolithic henge_

*Day Tours in the east of Dorset*

church dedicated to the Saxon saint Wolfrida. It was in Horton that Geoffrey of Monmouth was finally captured following his ill-fated rebellion in 1685. The duke had sensibly disguised himself as a yokel, but had neglected to dispose of his badge of the Order of the Garter. Horton is also home to a famous folly built in the mid 18th century and used in the filming of "Far from the Madding Crowd". Turn left to Chalbury Common [past the church] and in less than a mile turn right to Chalbury Hill. Here it is worth stopping at the picturesque white church, largely 18th century, but with some parts from the 13th century. There are lovely views across the Dorset countryside.

The road will lead back to the B3078 where you should turn right. Go past the Horton Inn and take the next left turn. Immediately on your right is the ruined church of Knowlton. This is one of the most atmospheric places in Dorset; a ruined Norman church set inside the bank and ditch of a Neolithic henge. There were in fact four henges here and a number of Bronze Age round burial barrows can be seen nearby. This was clearly a place of huge ceremonial significance in prehistoric times, some have compared it in scale to Stonehenge. The church served the small village of Knowlton, largely wiped out by the Black Death in medieval times.

Carry on the minor road until a T-junction; turn right to the village of Wimborne St. Giles. This, too, is a charming village, complete with 17th century almshouses next to the church. The village is the heart of the estate of one of the nation's most famous families, the Ashley-Coopers, Earls of Shaftesbury. The 7th Earl was one of the great Victorian Parliamentarians and champion of the poor. He campaigned tirelessly for better working conditions and was responsible for abolishing chimney sweeping by boys. The lovely mansion is in the centre of a huge park, well hidden from view. As you enter the village look out for the ancient village stocks by the roadside. From Wimborne St. Giles it is a short drive back to Cranborne, the start of our tour.

*Below: The lovely little church at Chalbury near Horton.*

*Day Tours in the east of Dorset*

*Above: Alderholt Mill is a great place for a cream tea.*

Historical Notes:

This area of Dorset is littered with the remains of ancient times. On the chalk downland on either side of the A354 it is difficult to miss the numerous Bronze Age round barrows. These were tombs, usually constructed of stone and then covered with earth. They were in use for well over a thousand years from about 2000 BC. Most have been excavated and have provided us with much information about life in those times. Unfortunately, much information has also been lost due to unscrupulous Victorian landowners who dug up many of the barrows looking for treasure. Some did indeed contain valuable items; it is thought these tombs may have been the last resting places of tribal chieftains.

One landowner, however, did excavate responsibly, uncovering a vast amount of information. This was General Pitt-Rivers, master of the vast Rushmore estate and generally regarded as the father of modern archaeology. There is an excellent section describing his work in Salisbury and South Wiltshire Museum in The Close, Salisbury, opposite the cathedral.

Ackling Dyke is a wonderful example of a Roman road. These roads were constructed very simply. Two ditches were dug with the material being thrown up in the middle to form a central platform known as an "agger". This was then paved and lined with kerbstones. It is the raised agger that forms Ackling Dyke. It is possible to walk along it in either direction. If you walk south you will see many round barrows in the fields to either side. Also in this area, although not visible from ground level, is the mysterious Dorset Cursus. This is a Neolithic structure over 4000 years old, consisting originally of two parallel earth banks which ran for a number of miles. It may have been some sort of processional way used in religious ceremonies.

Equally enigmatic is Bokerley Dyke, still a hugely impressive feature of the landscape. This is thought to have been a defensive earthwork against the looming Saxon threat following the Roman withdrawal. This is a fascinating period of history which saw huge changes in society.

Following the Norman conquest Cranborne Chase became a favourite hunting area for the kings and nobility. We should be thankful for this, for it has meant that the remains of our ancient past have been left relatively undisturbed. In other areas, years of cultivation have obliterated many of the round barrows and older long barrows.

*Below: A wild orchid flowers in a meadow in Alderholt and right, the quaint village sign in Wimborne St. Giles.*

*Places to eat and drink*

*In Cranborne try the **Fleur de Lys** or the **Sheath of Arrows**.*

*Although Martin has no pub, Damerham makes up for it with the **Compasses**. This pub has a delightful garden backing on to the village cricket pitch with the old Saxon church behind.*

***Alderholt Mill** is open for cream teas on weekend afternoons in the summer; sit and relax by the mill stream.*

*Alderholt itself has the **Churchill Arms**.*

*In Woodlands, just before Horton is **Kunei Indian Restaurant**.*

*When you reach Horton instead of turning right to the village, turn left and you will soon come to **Drusilla's Inn**, very popular locally.*

*Near Knowlton Circle is the **Horton Inn**. Turn right just past the bridge over the River Allen in Wimborne St. Giles and you will quickly find the **Bull Inn**.*

# Tour 2 - Blandford Forum

Length: 31 miles

OS map: 194

Roads: Some main roads, mostly easy B and minor roads.

Summary: Magnificent views and quaint villages.

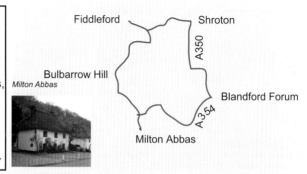

About 30 miles in length, this tour takes in some of Dorset's finest countryside and prettiest villages. There are walks to undertake for the energetic and plenty of possibilities for food and drink. It may seem odd to suggest two walks up steep hillforts that are adjacent, but both are magnificent. If you only have energy for one, choose Hambledon, especially if it is late afternoon or evening on a beautiful summer's day.

Blandford Forum is a pleasant place to start a tour. Having been largely destroyed by fire in the early 18th century it was completely rebuilt and is today one of the most complete Georgian market towns in England. Its prosperity grew from being an important route centre on a crossing point of the River Stour. It is still a thriving

*The Stour valley near Stourpaine.*

*Day Tours in the east of Dorset*

*Milton Abbey*

market town and home to one of England's most famous public schools, Bryanston. From Blandford we head north on the A350, past the village of Stourpaine and then turn next left on a minor road that runs between the two hillforts of Hod and Hambledon [signposted Hanford and Child Okeford]. There is a parking space on the left at GR 854112. A path leads up the impressive Iron Age bastion of Hod Hill. On top it is possible to walk all the way around the ramparts and admire the wonderful views of the Stour valley.

Hod Hill has an interesting history. In AD 43 a Roman legion under the command of the future emperor Vespasian defeated the local Durotriges here in one of many similar battles. There is evidence that the Romans had identified the hut of the British chieftain and subjected it to an onslaught of fire from their artillery, giant catapults firing crossbow type bolts. The chief was killed and the remaining tribesmen quickly surrendered after this demonstration of firepower. The Romans used the north-west corner of the hill to build a legionary fort, the earthworks of which are easily visible from the air. In early summer it is a delightful place to walk among carpets of wild flowers.

Another hillfort is the next stop on our tour; just a little further up the road it is possible to park by a path [lookout for a layby with a post box] that leads up Hambledon Hill [GR 845117]. This must be the one of the most beautiful and idyllic settings for any of these Iron Age settlements. Carved into the side of the hill, the formidable ramparts follow the contours on the western side, offering a magical vista when the sun is setting on a summer's evening.

*Hod Hill*

Hambledon consists of a number of spurs and has evidence of earlier habitation than its Iron Age remains. On the southern plateau was a Neolithic causewayed camp, one of the earliest human constructions. Some of these camps were not thought to be permanent settlements but perhaps ceremonial and trading centres. Many centuries later, during the

*Day Tours in the east of Dorset*

*The magnificent Iron Age hillfort at Hambledon Hill.*

English Civil War the hill was the scene of a minor battle between Cromwell's men and the "Dorset Clubmen", a mixed group of Dorset folk who were sick of the war and decided to take on both sides. They were quickly routed and treated leniently but dismissively by Cromwell.

The road leads through the village of Child Okeford, a large, thriving village where in the 16th century the local vicar wrote the famous hymn "All people that on earth do dwell". Turn left towards Shillingstone near the start of the village and you will soon join the A357 to Sturminster Newton, having first crossed over the River Stour. You might wish to explore Child Okeford first: it has a pretty centre with an interesting war memorial and a creeper clad pub. There are a couple of village stores to buy provisions.

Just before Sturminster Newton is Fiddleford Mill, a charming and working water mill on the River Stour. There is a right turn just after the Fiddleford Inn. The mill is open on Saturday, Sunday, Monday and Thursday between April and October and also offers bed and breakfast accommodation. The manor house nearby is also open to the public and is one of the oldest buildings in Dorset.

From Fiddleford go back along the A357 for about a kilometre and turn right to Okeford Fitzpaine. This is one of Dorset's prettiest villages, with twenty five of the 18th century buildings being listed.

From Okeford Fitzpaine the road leads up the chalk escarpment. Follow the signs to Bulbarrow. This hill gets its name from a Bronze Age "bowl barrow" situated on the summit. You can park on the left at the top or bear right at the road junction and park immediately on the right in Wooland Hill picnic site. The views from here

*Below: The view from Bulbarrow*

*Day Tours in the east of Dorset*

are breathtaking; you are at 900 feet above sea level and on a rare remnant of chalk heathland. It is only a short walk down the road to another pretty hillfort, Rawlsbury Camp at GR 768058. Bulbarrow was one of Thomas Hardy's favourite spots and features in "Tess of the D'Urbervilles".

Leave the car park and take the road that leads south-east towards Winterbourne Stickland, then bear right to Milton Abbas, one of Dorset's most famous villages. After entering the village, turn right towards Milton Abbey and this will lead you through the quaint main street of the village.

A prosperous market town once existed here, rivalling Blandford Forum, but in 1787 the first Earl of Dorchester, whose land it was and whose new mansion was nearby, decided he didn't like the noise and smell of the town so had it destroyed and a new one built further away. It was England's first planned new town and its uniform, square, thatched cottages are a well known sight on postcards and chocolate boxes. Today it presents a charming picture of English village life, but it is doubtful whether the usurped original residents thought so!

The Earl had constructed his new stately home on the site of the old Milton Abbey, originally founded by King Athelstan in AD 938. Although the house was built in 1771, the old abbey church dates from the 15th century. The grounds were landscaped by Capability Brown and the site is now a famous public school. It is possible to visit the abbey and enjoy the spectacular setting. At the bottom of the main street turn right to the school and abbey. Visitors can park near and visit the abbey or there is a footpath that starts on the left by a thatched cottage and leads to the abbey.

Go back up through the village, turn right to Winterborne Whitechurch and rejoin the A354 back to Blandford.

_Places to eat and drink_

_There are plenty of pubs, restaurants and cafés in Blandford, and this is a tour where there are also plenty of pubs along the way._

_The first you meet is the **White Horse** at Stourpaine. Slightly off the route but well worth a visit is the well known **Cricketers** at Shroton [or Iwerne Courtney]. You need to keep straight on instead of turning left for Shillingstone. This pub has lots of cricketing memorabilia and is a popular eating place._

_In Child Okeford the pretty **Bakers Arms** sits opposite the church, while on the road to Sturminster Newton the **Fiddleford Inn** has a nice garden._

_Okeford Fitzpaine has the **Royal Oak** while the thatched **Hambro Arms** is situated in the quaint main street of Milton Abbas._

_Finally, on your way back, you pass the **Milton Arms** in Winterborne Whitechurch just as you join the main road to Blandford._

# Tour 3 - Shaftesbury

Length: 26 miles

OS map: 184

Roads: B and minor roads mainly, easy and usually quiet.

Summary: Some less well known treasures.

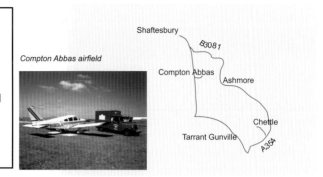

Compton Abbas airfield

This is a relatively short tour of only twenty-six miles, but it includes a variety of attractions to visit and some wonderful scenery. It can be done as a gentle drive with perhaps a stop for refreshments, or a longer tour, taking time to visit and explore some of the places en route.

Situated on the edge of the chalk escarpment overlooking the Blackmore Vale, Shaftesbury is a picturesque and relatively unspoilt market town. It grew following the founding of an abbey there by Alfred the Great around 880 AD; his daughter was the first abbess. Today, Shaftesbury is perhaps most famous for Gold Hill, the quaint, steep, cobbled street that appears on countless tourist brochures and postcards, and

*Below: Gold Hill in Shaftesbury. Above right: Fontmell Down*

*Day Tours in the east of Dorset*

which notably featured on a Hovis advert. The Gold Hill Fair takes place in July and is one of the county's premier open air events. At the top of Gold Hill, behind the town hall, is Shaftesbury Museum. Once the town's doss house it now contains many objects of local interest.

Adjacent to Gold Hill are the remains of the old abbey, founded by Alfred the Great, who made his daughter the first abbess. Not much is left, but a museum and pretty garden enhance the meagre stonework. Outside the abbey is a quiet terrace with lovely views across the vale. The abbey became famous in the tenth century when it became the resting place of King Edward the Martyr, the young successor to Edgar, brutally murdered at Corfe Castle by his stepmother's followers so that her son Ethelred [the Unready] could take the throne. It soon grew into a place of pilgrimage and acquired considerable wealth. King Edward is no longer here but a memorial in the abbey grounds marks where his tomb used to be.

Leave Shaftesbury on the A30 eastwards, then immediately turn south on the B3081. Go through Melbury Abbas up on to the chalk downland. There is parking here and you can walk on the lovely, National Trust owned Fontmell Down, with spectacular views over the Dorset countryside to the west. Nearby is the perfect place for lunch or a snack, the busy little airfield of Compton Abbas [Grid Square 8918]. Here a variety of small aircraft come and go on the grass runway, overlooked by the terrace of the excellent café.

Continue south past Fontmell Down and after about three miles turn left at the crossroads at Hill Farm and take the road that follows the course of the Tarrant, a

typical chalk stream that gives its name to several villages. The first of these is Tarrant Gunville, a pretty place strung out along the stream. As you leave the village look out for the gatehouse of Eastbury House, once one of the greatest mansions in the whole of England, built in the early 18th century by wealthy industrialist George Bubb with the intention of rivalling Blenheim Palace and, like Blenheim and Castle Howard, designed by Vanbrugh. Not much remains of the house: after his death the house was too expensive for anyone to maintain and it was largely dismantled. Legend has it that the ghost of Bubb's dishonest butler haunts the gatehouse, riding in on a headless horse, and that he has become one of the undead, a vampire!

The Tarrant eventually leads to the main Salisbury – Blandford road, the A354, at Tarrant Hinton. Turn left here and then shortly left again to the small village and manor house at Chettle. Again built in the early 1700s, this is a classic Queen Anne house and was the home of George Chafin, the Ranger of Cranborne Chase. The house and its gardens are open to the public on the first Sunday of each month from Easter to September. It is possible to enjoy the surroundings of Eastbury and Chettle from the footpaths that start at or near Tarrant Gunville [two start at GR 927128 and GR 935121, OS sheet 195 or Explorer sheet 118].

We now take the A354 towards Blandford before turning left at Thickthorne Cross.

*Above: The homely manor of Chettle, seeen from the footpath at the front of the house.*

*Right: Ashmore, the highest village in Dorset.*

*Day Tours in the east of Dorset*

To the south of the main road here is Thickthorne Down where the enigmatic Dorset Cursus starts. This is a Neolithic structure, thought to have been an important ceremonial way. Nothing can be seen of the Cursus from the ground but several impressive long barrows are visible.

Continue along this minor road towards the village of Ashmore, turning left again after about half a mile. The road leads past the Larmer Tree gardens. It is worth a short detour here to explore these enchanting Victorian gardens created by the father of British archaeology, General Pitt-Rivers. The gardens are actually in Wiltshire, the Larmer Tree itself marking the boundary between the two counties. They were created in 1880 for the recreation of estate workers and the general public. They proved very popular; thousands promenaded and picnicked in the grounds. The general, who had inherited the vast Rushmore estate, even provided free crockery and cutlery for visitors to use! Nowadays the café and restaurant offer meals and cream teas in genteel surroundings. The gardens are open from Easter Sunday to the end of September, every day except Fridays and Saturdays.

Continue on to the village of Ashmore, the highest in Dorset at 700 feet above sea level. The centre of the village is a circular pond that, somewhat mysteriously at that altitude, never seems to dry up. The pond must have been the reason for the village's beginning in Roman times. It is a lovely place to wander, off the beaten track, with mellow stone buildings reflected in the still waters of the pond. The lanes around the village are tranquil and offer lovely views over Cranborne Chase, together with, in summer, masses of wild flowers.

From Ashmore rejoin the B3081 which will take you back to Shaftesbury via the aptly named zig-zag hill, again enjoying far-reaching views from the edge of the chalk escarpment.

*Places to eat and drink*

*Shaftesbury has a number of pubs, hotels and restaurants within an easy stroll of the car park in the centre of town.*

*For a different atmosphere try the excellent licensed restaurant at* **Compton Abbas Airfield.** *It serves snacks as well as meals in a unique setting.*

*Pubs are notably missing from the route this tour takes but several can be found with short detours. When coming to the main Blandford road at Tarrant Hinton go straight across to follow the course of the Tarrant. You will shortly come to Tarrant Monkton where you will find the popular* **Langton Arms,** *with bar food and a restaurant.*

*Carrying on up the Blandford road past the suggested turning to the Larmer Tree Gardens will soon bring you to the* **Inn on the Chase** *at Cashmoor.*

*If you visit the* **Larmer Tree Gardens** *it is well worthwhile using the restaurant there. In a lovely setting and with tasteful décor, it undoubtedly retains the character and atmosphere General Pitt-Rivers intended for the gardens.*

# Tour 4 - Wareham and Corfe Castle

Length: 28 miles

OS Map: 195

Roads: Mainly B roads, generally easy.

Summary: History, spectacular coastal scenery and lovely Portland and Purbeck stone.

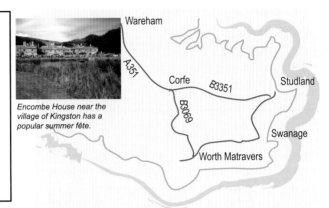

*Encombe House near the village of Kingston has a popular summer fête.*

There is much to see on this tour. Again it passes through quaint villages and offers stunning scenery, but it is well worth the effort getting out and walking to some of the places suggested, particularly those on the coast. Taking in all the sites and doing all the suggested walks may prove difficult in a day.

We start in the ancient town of Wareham, sandwiched between the Rivers Piddle and Frome. It was here in the 9th century that Alfred the Great built defences against the Viking invaders. In AD 876 Alfred's arch enemy, Guthrum, had established a base here, but later left to attack Exeter. The grass banks to the north of the town by the River Piddle are the remains of these Saxon defences; it is possible to walk along them. The heart of the town is Wareham Quay on the River Frome. From here you can walk along the riverside with its multitude of little boats and yachts.

The church of St. Mary's is largely 14th century and was the place where the body of the murdered Saxon King Edward was originally taken [see below]. Dorset's oldest church, St. Martin's, is situated in the middle of the north wall and is almost completely Saxon.

From Wareham head south along the A351 to what is probably Dorset's best known village, Corfe Castle, gateway to the "Isle of Purbeck". Here natural streams have cut through the chalk ridge providing the perfect place for a defended settlement. It was in use as such long before the present castle, which was built by the Normans.

There is a car park in the village and one just outside which is convenient for the castle. Once there it is rewarding to explore on foot. The village has lost none of its character and when the roads are quiet it really does feel as if you are stepping back in time. At the beginning and end of the day the sun can light up the castle and the village buildings of Portland Stone in an unforgettable manner. If you are lucky enough to visit at the right time you might find the castle encircled by a sea of mist, giving the impression it is an enchanted island!

From Corfe Castle take the road south towards Swanage, but turn right just outside the village to Kingston [B3069]. The road climbs up the ridge formed by the Portland and Purbeck limestones; on the way it is possible to stop and walk over Corfe Common, where there are lovely views of the village and castle.

Kingston is another unspoilt village made out of Portland Stone. Its main point of interest is its large Victorian church, built in the 1870s by the 3rd Earl of Eldon. There are, in fact, two 19th century churches in Kingston although only one is now used as such. The earl felt obliged to have one built that matched his own power and standing. It was built with local stone and by local craftsmen, providing work at a low time for the quarrying industry. It dominates the village, which, with its stone cottages and creeper clad pub, has become one of the landmarks of the Isle of Purbeck.

Follow the B3069 out of the village towards Swanage. After about a mile turn right down the minor road to Worth Matravers. There is a car park on the right just as you enter the village. This is a popular location; at weekends the car park is packed with walkers who come to enjoy the many coastal paths accessed from here. The village itself is lovely, with a central green and duck pond surrounded by cottages built from Portland Stone.

There is much history associated with this peaceful corner of the Purbecks. Since Roman times the Portland Stone has been quarried and it is worth a short walk down

*Below: The village pond in Worth Matravers.*

*Above: Wareham Quay is a popular place to relax in the sunshine.*

to the coast to Winspit [GR 977761], where huge caves bear testament to the amount of stone removed over the years. It is a beautiful spot and one can only wonder at the danger of loading the huge blocks of stone onto barges anchored offshore. In 1786 Winspit was the scene of a terrible sea disaster when a fine East Indiaman called the Halsewell got into difficulty in stormy weather and was driven in to the rocks. Although about 160 died, the local quarrymen received much praise for their bravery in a rescue effort that went on for twenty-four hours.

In the village churchyard is the grave of a local farmer called Benjamin Jesty who inoculated his wife and family against smallpox in 1774, twenty-four years before Edward Jenner proposed that this was a way to combat disease. It was also here that, in the 1930s, secret tests took place in fields near the village that helped develop radar.

The village is an ideal place to begin a coastal walk; as well as Winspit, try the path that leads west from the village to St. Aldhelm's Head with its coastguard station and Norman chapel. There is a car park at the end of the road that leads from the village [GR 964774]. There are two routes to the headland, the one that hugs the coast offers some of the most stunning views of the Jurassic Coast anywhere in Dorset, but beware of a steep dip and climb across a dry valley at one point.

Rejoin the B3069 and follow it into Swanage. This is an old fashioned, family seaside resort set in a bay carved out of the soft rocks sandwiched by the Chalk and

the Portland and Purbeck limestones. It has a long sea front and a good beach. There is a large car park at the southern end of the town from where it is an easy stroll to Peveril Point with its coastguard lookout station [GR 041787]. The thin layers of the Purbeck Limestone here were formed in tropical swamps where dinosaurs once roamed. On the flat surfaces of the harder layers footprints of these creatures are sometimes found. It is also possible to walk or drive to Durlston Head [GR 035773], now a country park and with an easy and magnificent walk along the cliffs to the lighthouse at Anvil Point.

From Swanage take the minor road north through Ulwell to Studland. This is an unusual village, tucked away at the foot of the chalk ridge and pressed against the sea by the open expanse of Studland Heath. In season you will need to park in one of the National Trust car parks that provide access to the beach. This is one of the best swimming beaches in Dorset and the coast path leads all the way along to South Haven Point at the entrance to Poole Harbour. Many footpaths lead across the heath from where there are views across Poole Harbour. Look out for the giant Agglestone, a huge block of iron rich sandstone, reputedly thrown there by the Devil, but actually a natural product of the weathering process!

The B3352 will take you back towards Corfe Castle. There is opportunity to park and again admire the wide ranging views over the heathland and the harbour. From Corfe Castle follow the road back to Wareham. The total distance is about 28 miles.

*Above left: The horizontally bedded Portland and Purbeck limestones at Winspit.*

Historical Notes

Saxons and Vikings

In the ninth century England faced growing numbers of raids from Viking longships. These were no longer "smash and grab" raids; the Danes had their sights set on conquest. The Saxon kingdoms with their peasant armies were often no match for the well trained Vikings. Fortunately for Wessex, a young king of extraordinary resourcefulness was eventually to defeat the Danes and usher in an age of peace and prosperity: he was, of course, Alfred the Great.

We can only imagine what it must have been like to live in those times with the constant threat of violence, relying on lookouts to warn of the invaders' approach, and being ready to leave at a moment's notice. The Isle of Purbeck was much affected by these raids with Wareham being a particular trouble spot. It remains the highest point

*The impressive remains of Corfe Castle continue to dominate the Purbeck landscape.*

*Day Tours in the east of Dorset*

of navigation on the River Frome. Viking ships could reach here after sailing through Poole harbour; they would then be free to plunder the rich countryside around. Alfred recognised the threat and built strong defences around the town. These are the Saxon walls that can still be seen. However, they didn't stop Alfred's arch enemy Guthrum from occupying the town in 876. Perhaps an indication of how war weary the men of Wessex had become or perhaps a part of Alfred's grand strategy, the Saxons merely shadowed the Danes until they moved on in the Spring.

The Viking threat was largely removed in 877 when a large naval battle took place off Swanage. Aided by a storm, the English ships were victorious and around 120 Viking ships were sunk.

Edward the Martyr

"No worse deed than this was ever done by the English since they first sought the land of Britain." This is how the Anglo-Saxon Chronicles describes the murder of King Edward at Corfe Castle in March 978. It was a heinous crime that shocked the nation and gave birth to a legend; that of King Edward "the Martyr", later to become Saint Edward.

Edward was the eldest son of King Edgar, one of the greatest Saxon kings who established an era of unprecedented peace and prosperity following the removal of the Viking threat by Alfred. Danish subjects lived at peace with the English and churches and monasteries flourished under Archbishop Dunstan.

Edgar died in 975 and was succeeded by his handsome eldest son, born to his first wife. According to legend, Edward was kind, popular and guided by wise counsel. Edward's wicked stepmother, Edgar's second wife Aelfthryth, wanted her son Ethelred to succeed Edgar.

Corfe had been a natural defensive position, atop its natural hill in the only gap in the chalk ridge. As Viking raids diminished it had become a popular royal hunting retreat. In March 978 this is what the young king was doing when he decided to call on his stepmother who was staying in Corfe. Relations between the two seem to have been good, at least on the surface, and Edward was welcomed with due civility. Before he had dismounted, however, he had been stabbed in the back several times. He died quickly and was thrown down a well. About a year later the body was recovered and taken to St. Mary's church in Wareham. Stories of miraculous healing grew up around the well and the legend of Edward "the Martyr" had begun. His body was eventually taken to Shaftesbury where an abbey founded by Alfred grew rich as a place of pilgrimage.

As is often the case, the legend bears only a passing resemblance to reality. As a child, Edward was renowned for his temper and was not popular. Little is known of his short reign, but it seems things soon began to go wrong. In 976 there was a great famine and signs of more widespread disorder. Perhaps if his half brother who succeeded him had become a great king there would be no legend of Saint Edward. Unfortunately for England, Ethelred was not a success and has become known to later generations as the "Unready".

Corfe Castle

Following the defeat of the Vikings in the naval battle off Swanage, Alfred built a castle at Corfe. As we have seen, it occupies a notorious place in Saxon history. After the Norman conquest it became a royal palace and was a favourite with King John who kept his crown jewels there. He famously used it as a prison for French captives, starving twenty-two of them to death here. It also became a useful place to keep treasure due to its remote location, strategic position and massive walls.

During the civil war between King Stephen and the Empress Matilda it was besieged by the king's forces, but not taken. Throughout the medieval period it continued to be a royal palace until it was sold by Queen Elizabeth to her Chancellor. He in turn sold it to the powerful Bankes family.

During the Civil War Sir John Bankes was the Lord Chief Justice to King Charles I and it was left to Lady Bankes to defend the castle against Parliamentary forces in 1643 and again in 1645. She proved a formidable opponent and was only defeated due to the treachery of one of her own men. The life of the castle came to a tragic end in 1646, when after a three year siege by Parliament forces, the castle finally fell and Parliament ordered its destruction. The ruins you see today are the result of that destruction: the fact that it took three months to destroy bears witness to its strength. Most of the village was rebuilt around this time using much of the stone from the castle. Thus the village retains a very original and homogeneous feel, adding to the charm of its location.

## Places to eat and drink

*Wareham has plenty to offer in terms of pubs, restaurants and hotels. Those on the quay, the* **Old Granary** *and* **The Quay** *have a lovely setting. There are also many take-aways.*

*Those looking for character are spoilt for choice on this tour. In Corfe Castle the* **Greyhound** *and* **Bankes Arms** *are well placed in the centre of the village, but wander the streets for smaller, more intimate places.*

*At Kingston the* **Scott Arms** *serves good food accompanied by spectacular views of the castle. It would be difficult to find a better pub garden anywhere in Dorset.*

*The* **Square and Compass** *at Worth Matravers is justifiably popular with walkers.*

*Swanage has many pubs, cafés and restaurants, some with sea views. Good fish and chips are also available on the sea front.*

# Tour 5 - Bere Regis

Length: 40 miles

OS Map: 194

Roads: Quiet minor and B roads.

Summary: Lots to see and do.

*Bere Regis church*

There is much to see and do on this tour. As well as stunning natural sights there are interesting churches and houses. Several large tourist attractions will also compete for your time. You may wish to return to some of them at a later date, or simply decide which you are going to visit before setting off.

Bere Regis is now a small place by-passed by the main road. It started as a Saxon village but grew in size and importance thanks to royal patronage and its annual fair that became one of the biggest and most popular in southern England.

It was home to Simon de Montfort one of the fathers of the English Parliament, but perhaps more famously the rich and powerful Turberville family, inspiration for Thomas Hardy's D'Urbervilles. In the beautiful 15th century church is the family tomb and the magnificent Turberville stained glass window.

Leave Bere Regis going west on the A35 and in just over two miles turn left on the B3390 towards Affpuddle, crossing the River Piddle. Just after Affpuddle it is worth taking a short detour left to the village of Briantspuddle. This village gets its name from Brian de Turberville, lord of the manor in the reign of Edward III. It is interesting in that it was developed by Sir Ernest Debenham, a wealthy London draper, with the idea of becoming a model, self-sufficient estate. Today it retains an air of ordered peacefulness. There is also an interesting war memorial.

Rejoin the B3390 and shortly take another left turn to the village of Moreton. Here is one of Dorset's hidden treasures. The church was unluckily hit by a returning German bomber in World War II and all of its beautiful stained glass windows were destroyed. They were replaced by a wonderful series of engraved windows by Laurence Whistler.

The church held the funeral of Lawrence of Arabia who was killed nearby in a road accident. He is buried in the new churchyard.

From Moreton head south-east along the minor road to Wool. Near the ancient bridge over the River Frome is Woolbridge Manor, seat of the Turberville family. Legend has it that a ghostly coach and horses haunts the bridge, but can only be seen by those who have Turberville blood in their veins.

From Wool we head south along the B3071 to one of Dorset's best known beauty spots, Lulworth Cove. There is a large car park here from where one can explore the lovely coastline either east or west. Go westwards over the headland to see Durdle Door, a much photographed arch, cut by the sea through the Purbeck Limestone.

In the other direction is the famous cove itself, another marvel of Nature created by erosion. A river has worn a gap through the hard Portland and Purbeck limestones, allowing the sea to break through and wear away at the softer rocks behind. Apart from the cove, do not miss two other adjacent sites, arguably even more impressive. On the east side of the cove follow the coast path to the "Fossil Forest". Here, on a ledge on the cliffs, are the remains of the fossilised stumps of trees that lived about 150 million years ago. These trees grew in swamps where dinosaurs waded. The stumps of the trees were colonised by algae and it is the remains of these that are fossilised. They are known as stromatolites.

On the west side of Lulworth Cove is Stair Hole. This is a mini version of the main cove where a small gap has been eroded in the limestones and the sea is beginning to hollow out another bay. In the cliff on the east of Stair Hole is the famous Lulworth

*Lulworth Cove*

*Day Tours in the east of Dorset*

*Above: The wonderful engraved windows in Moreton Church by Laurence Whistler.*

Crumple. Here, the originally flat lying, strata have been folded by huge earth movements into contorted shapes. These were part of the mountain building episode that led to the formation of the Alps.

Head north again on the B3070, following it through Lulworth Camp to the village of East Lulworth. Here you can visit Lulworth Castle. Originally a mock castle built as a hunting lodge in the early 16th century, it was acquired by Humphrey Weld and subsequently became the centre of his estate. The castle suffered a terrible fire in 1929 and has not been used as a home since. It has been repaired, however, and is now open to the public. The Weld family still own the estate and occupy a new manor completed in 1977. The house and grounds are open to the public on Wednesday afternoons in summer. A small minor road will take you from East Lulworth up the chalk escarpment to the south-east. This is army land, used as firing ranges, and is not always open to the public. However, it is open almost every weekend and every day in school holidays. The times of opening can be found on www.lulworth.com/ranges. htm or by ringing 01929 462721 ext. 4819. Follow the road up the hill and perhaps stop at the viewpoint [GR 887812] to admire the Dorset coastline. Carry further along this small road and you will see a sharp turning down a narrow road to the deserted village of Tyneham.

This is one of Dorset's best kept secrets; a charming relic of a bygone age, set in beautiful scenery and completely free! The story of Tyneham is well documented:

taken over by the army in 1943 to be used as part of the preparations for D-Day, it was never returned to the villagers as originally promised. The tiny cottages now stand ruined, but the church and schoolroom have been preserved. The skeleton of the old rectory and the remains of its once impressive garden indicate the standing village priests once had.

A path leads from the village down to the sea at Worbarrow Bay. Like Lulworth it has been scoured out of the soft rocks between the Portland and Purbeck limestones and the Chalk. It is possible to walk up the coast path to the south and around back to Tyneham – well worth it if you can stand the climb.

Rejoin the road along the chalk ridge and follow it eastwards until you see a turn on the right to Kimmeridge. Carry on until you reach Kimmeridge Bay; you will have to pay a toll in the holiday seasons. On first sight Kimmeridge may not seem the prettiest of seaside destinations, but it is an interesting place none the less. Hard rock ledges stretch out to sea forming fascinating patterns. The Romans made the hard Kimmeridge shale into jewellery and ornaments, but it has also been used since prehistoric times as a fuel. There have been a number of attempts to base local industries on this source of fuel.

Kimmeridge is now a marine nature reserve, providing one of the best diving sites on the southern coast.

Head back north, rejoining the minor road where you turned off. Follow that northwards towards Wareham. Go round the ring road towards Poole. After you have crossed the railway line turn left on a minor road towards Bere Regis that goes through Cold Harbour. *Below: Looking across Worbarrow Bay from the path on Gad Cliff.*

*Above: Clavell Tower overlooks Kimmeridge.*

## Places to eat and drink

*There are plenty of good pubs on this tour, but lovers of fresh air will find some wonderful places for getting the picnic hamper out.*

*In Bere Regis try the **Royal Oak** or the **Drax Arms**.*

*Just before you arrive in Wool, at East Burton, is the **Seven Stars**, a large family pub with a big garden.*

*Wool has the **Black Bear** and the **Ship**.*

*At Lulworth you will find the thatched **Castle Inn**, while at the Cove itself is the **Lulworth Cove Inn** and a large café at the **Heritage Centre**. East Lulworth has the **Weld Arms**.*

***Whiteway Hill** is a wonderful place for a picnic with breathtaking views of the Purbeck coastline. Similarly the large grassy car park at **Tyneham** is an ideal place to put down the rug and get out the sandwiches.*

*For a different experience try the small **restaurant@kimmeridge**. Again, a great place for a picnic is the large car park overlooking Kimmeridge Bay.*

*Wareham has been mentioned previously in Tour 4, but just after you have left Wareham, at Cold Harbour, is the well known pub the **Silent Woman**.*

The Jurassic Coast

The 85 mile stretch of coastline from East Devon to Swanage is now a World Heritage Site. A beautiful and varied coastline, it was granted its status due to its importance geologically, having a unique record, in the rocks, of the development of life on earth.

The earliest rocks we see on the Jurassic Coast are around 250 million years old from the era known as the Triassic. At this time all the Earth's land was concentrated in one huge landmass called, by geologists, Pangaea. At the end of the previous geological era, the Permian, almost 95% of species on the Earth had become extinct. This is the greatest mass extinction in geological history and its cause is still a mystery.

In the eras that followed life blossomed again; new animals and plants developed including the dinosaurs and the ammonites. The rocks of the Dorset coast contain fossils of thousands of species that lived in shallow seas that teemed with life and in swamps on the edge of land where huge dinosaurs waded, the water helping to support their great weight. The rocks of the Isle of Purbeck were formed in the Jurassic and Cretaceous periods. As well as containing many fossils they also have an interesting structure, the result of huge earth movements that resulted in the Alpine mountain chain. There is not the space to go into great detail about the geology here but it is worth mentioning two locations specifically.

Lulworth Cove is famous for its interesting geology, but many people visit without appreciating even the basic facts. The cove has been formed because a river broke through the hard Portland and Purbeck rocks on the coast, allowing the sea to erode the softer clays and sands behind. The hard chalk at the back of the cove is more resistant and this has resulted in the shape of the cove. What some do not notice is that the Portland and Purbeck rocks, mainly limestones, have been tilted so that they are almost vertical. Remember that these are rocks laid down on the sea bed; the layers or strata were originally horizontal. Tremendous earth movements caused by the collision of continents has raised them and tilted them almost vertical. The softer rocks on top of them and consequently younger, have also been tilted, as has the still younger Chalk. The near vertical layers we see at Lulworth and elsewhere on the Isle of Purbeck represent the vertical limb of a giant "step fold". Imagine the rocks at the mouth of the cove rising upwards and then gradually becoming horizontal and extending out to sea. Now imagine the rocks behind and the Chalk doing the same thing – this is how it once was!

Kimmeridge is another famous site. The rocks here are Jurassic and were deposited in shallow, muddy seas teeming with life. The layers of the sediments here are relatively thin and this is mainly because as the sediments collected at the bottom of the ocean they squeezed those below. It has been estimated that the thickness of the sediment has been reduced by a factor of about eight. Looking at the cliffs now it is staggering to think how much material was originally deposited in these ancient seas!

# Other Places to Visit

Finally, here are some more places you might go for an interesting day out or for a shorter visit. They are in no particular order and I am not suggesting they form a tour: there is something to delight and enchant about all of them.

Christchurch

Built around a large natural harbour at the confluence of the Rivers Stour and Avon, Christchurch offers a number of places to enjoy the coastline. A walk up and around **Hengistbury Head** gives marvellous views across the harbour, of the Dorset coast and across to the Isle of Wight. Hengistbury was a major settlement in the Iron Age and the defensive ramparts from that time can still be seen. There is a large car park at GR 162910, OS sheet 195. From **Mudeford** [GR 188922] you can walk along by the sea to the busy harbour. There are a number of cafés on the sea front where you can sit and admire the views. Further east at GR 203931 is **Highcliffe Castle**. This is a Victorian mansion open to the public, where you can eat and drink in delightful grounds, walk along the cliffs through a nature reserve or go down to the beach.

Wimborne

Upstream on the River Stour from Christchurch, Wimborne is an ancient town with a magnificent twin-towered church, known as a Minster because it was originally the centre of a mission where evangelising clergy were based. The present church was built by the Normans on the site of an earlier Saxon place of worship. Head north-west from Wimborne on the B3082 and you will soon come to the Iron Age hillfort of **Badbury Rings**. This is a lovely place for a picnic and a walk. There are also occasionally point to point races here. Badbury is one of the places associated with the Battle of Badon Hill where legend has it King Arthur defeated the Saxons. It was almost certainly the site of a battle when the Romans invaded – that time the invaders won! Just south of Badbury at GR 958007 is the medieval **Whitemill Bridge** over the Stour. This is a charming spot with a mill owned by the National Trust and open during the summer. On a minor road near the village of Tarrant Rushton at GR 950061 you can experience the vast expanse of what used to be **Tarrant Rushton airfield**. It was from here in June 1944 that hundreds of gliders took off for Normandy, including those destined to land troops at the infamous Pegasus Bridge. There is a fitting memorial here and the place has a special atmosphere.

Poole and Bournemouth

The two biggest urban areas in Dorset, Poole and Bournemouth have many places with atmosphere along the coast and around the magnificent harbour that is the second largest in the world.

More places to see along the way......

*Above left: Medieval Whitemill Bridge over the River Stour at Sturminster Marshall.*

*Above right: The famous Beech avenue near Badbury Rings.*

*Left: Winspit on the Isle of Purbeck.*

*Above left: Lobster pots on Mudeford's busy quay. Above right: Looking across to Chapman's Pool from the path to St. Aldhelm's Head.*